CATHOLIC
COMMON GROUND INITIATIVE

CATHOLIC
COMMON
GROUND
INITIATIVE

Foundational Documents

CARDINAL JOSEPH BERNARDIN
& ARCHBISHOP OSCAR H. LIPSCOMB

Introduction by
Philip J. Murnion

A Crossroad Herder Book
The Crossroad Publishing Company
New York

1997

The Crossroad Publishing Company
370 Lexington Avenue, New York, NY 10017

Copyright ©1997 by National Pastoral Life Center

Printed in the United States of America

Library of Congress Cataloging-in-Publication Data

Bernardin, Joseph Louis, 1928–96
     Catholic Common Ground Initiative : foundational
documents / Joseph Bernardin and Oscar H. Lipscomb ;
introduction by Philip J. Murnion.
          p.   cm.
     "A Crossroad Herder Book."
     Prepared by the National Pastoral Life Center.
     Includes bibliographical references.
     ISBN 0-8245-1716-4 (pbk.)
     1. Catholic Common Ground Initiative—History—
Sources. 2. Catholic Church—United States—History—
20th century. I. Lipscomb, Oscar H.   II. National
Pastoral Life Center (U.S.)   III. Title.
BX1404.B47   1997
282'.73'09049—dc21   97-15613
                                                                    CIP

CONTENTS

INTRODUCTION

Philip J. Murnion

"Will the Catholic Church in the United States enter the new millennium as a church of promise, augmented by the faith of rising generations and able to be a leavening force in our culture?" This question opens the statement, "Called to Be Catholic: Church in a Time of Peril." The subject: the Catholic Church in the United States. The hope: that the church can be a leavening force in our culture. The condition: the faith of new generations of Catholics. It is the church as an instrument of the reign of God in the world and not only as a community of compassion and consolation, however essential these are to the Christian community, that is the concern of the statement.

To relate to the new millennium is to situate the concern in the context of particular times and circumstances, not simply of the perennial challenges of faithful discipleship, acknowledging that the entrance of Christ into this world continues to give significance to the particularities of time and Christ's mission to this world.

What would hinder the church from fulfilling its mission? What is required for carrying out this mission? The statement points to a number of interwoven strands of difficulty facing the church: polarization among its leaders; a sense of disenfranchisement and confusion about beliefs among its members, particularly the young; and uncertainty about identity in many Catholic institutions. Among these, polarization is given particular attention, a polarization that "inhibits discussion and cripples leadership." Implicitly, therefore, it is the condition of church leadership as it addresses the pastoral challenges of the day that receives special attention.

What is required to correct the situation and strengthen the church's approach to its mission? "American Catholics must reconstitute the conditions for addressing our differences constructively—a common ground centered on faith in Jesus, marked by accountability to the living Catholic tradition, and ruled by a renewed spirit of civility, dialogue, generosity, and broad and serious consultation." This is the program proposed by the statement: an effort truly Catholic in its commitment to the Lord and responsibility to the church, one open to all the ways in which we try to understand what the Lord has revealed and what the world is saying—"all the gifts of wisdom and understanding in the church"—with the goal of being constructive. The aim is pastoral: strengthening the church for its mission in the new millennium.

The statement was released by Cardinal Joseph Bernardin at a press conference on August 12, 1996, when he also announced the formation of the Catholic Common Ground Project. (The name was changed two months later to the Catholic Common Ground Initiative, with the understanding that "project" could suggest a specific task to be completed, as it were, by a task force, while "initiative" connotes stimulus to a whole way of acting that could inspire many projects, tasks, and communities in the church. I will employ the final title from here on.) A large number of representatives of the electronic and print media—church and secular—showed up for the press conference. Undoubtedly, this was a tribute to Cardinal Bernardin's prominence, his ongoing open relationship with the press, and the expectation that the subject must be important to him, suffering as he was from the ravages of cancer.

The reaction was powerful. The statement quickly spread throughout the church. Within a couple of months there were perhaps three to four hundred thousand copies of the statement in print; it was carried in whole or part in any number of newspapers and magazines, and almost two thousand people downloaded the statement from the electronic "home page" of the Archdiocese of Chicago. (Since then the statement has also been translated into Spanish, and a German version has been circulated among church leaders in Switzerland, Germany, and Austria.) Editorials and op-ed pieces appeared in Catholic newspapers and magazines as well as in the *Philadelphia Inquirer* and the *Boston Globe* and other secular newspapers. Network television news programs carried stories, as did National Public Radio and other radio networks and stations. Within a short time, hundreds and hundreds of people wrote letters to Cardinal Bernardin and to the National Pastoral Life Center. What captured considerable attention was the acknowledgment of a problem of discourse in the church (problems elicit more media interest than promises), the bold call for dialogue about thorny issues, and, to be sure, the criticism publicly leveled against the statement and, to a somewhat lesser degree, the Initiative itself by four of Cardinal Bernardin's fellow cardinals. Such public criticism of a cardinal by fellow cardinals was unusual if not unprecedented. I will discuss the reactions further, but for the present it is enough to say that something about the statement and the proposed Initiative sparked enormous interest within the church and in the larger culture. It touched some nerve, stimulating excitement in many, fear in a few.

Where did this come from, what did it all mean?

PASTORAL ORIGINS OF THE INITIATIVE

A CHRONOLOGY CAN provide the context for understanding the statement and the Initiative. It is the chronology of a process but also of a man, Cardinal Bernardin. The two are intimately linked.

In 1992, Cardinal Bernardin distributed to the parishes of the Archdiocese of Chicago a short reflection on the mission of the parish entitled *The Parish in the Contemporary Church*. In doing so he did not follow his usual practice. Typically, when the Cardinal was preparing a statement for the church of Chicago or for presentation to the conference of bishops, the statement would go through a number of drafts as it was guided through a lengthy process of consultation. This time he surprised his staff with the statement and directed that it be distributed throughout the church of Chicago as a booklet simply reproduced from the typescript.

It is a modest statement, unsurprising in its analysis but quite focused in its appeal. The statement focuses particularly on the role of the priest. The Cardinal addresses concerns of parish liturgy and preaching, parochial schools and religious education programs, ministry to young people, and the sharing of all ministries with both parishioners and new members of parish staffs. Throughout the pastoral, he addresses the relationships between priest and people in regard to these areas of church life and emphasizes the need to combine faithfulness to the church's doctrinal and pastoral norms with respect for the many differences among people and views of Catholic life. Typical is the statement: "I see no opposition between a dynamic parish liturgical program and popular devotions, old and new." In effect, the pastoral calls for fostering in parishes what the Cardinal would later call an authentic common ground, faithful to the demands of church teaching and hospitable to the varieties of ways in which that teaching can be lived out in a community of Catholics.

Cardinal Bernardin also sent the statement as a courtesy to me at the National Pastoral Life Center because the center is devoted to parish life in the United States. (The center originated in the Parish Project of the National Conference of Catholic Bishops, but since 1983 has operated as an independent service to the nation's Catholic parishes.) In correspondence and conversations that followed between Cardinal Bernardin and me, we discussed how pastoral concerns such as those he addressed in his statement were often obscured by increasing polarization among individuals, groups, and organizations in the church. Differences of opinion are inevitable and even essential, but it seems that too often the expression of differences descends into an accusatory–defensive cycle, casting doubts on the basic faithfulness or openness of the disputing parties. "Parties" was a word that seemed to describe the situation. Not that there were two or three or more clearly defined groups that could be identified in party terms: the competing groups and views varied somewhat with the subject. At the heart of the matter was the concern that church leaders were not adequately addressing serious pastoral concerns: concerns about our worship and religious education, the church's social and pastoral ministry, the dramatic changes in the numbers of priests and sisters serving the church, and the numbers of lay people assuming increased responsibility for the church's pastoral ministry, to name but a few issues.

HOW COULD WE understand what was happening? The decision was made to gather people simply to discuss the situation. No plan, no goal, no commitment to anything more than one meeting. That was the basis of an invitation to a group of people—a few bishops, some priests in both pastoral and academic work, sisters, lay people who were directly involved in church ministry and others who were not, people who had some involvement with the National Pastoral Life Center's publications and projects. The first meeting lasted a day and a half. The discussion was wide-ranging, all around the twin concerns of serious issues inadequately addressed and the poverty, if not polarization, in current church discourse. Those present agreed that continuing discussion was of interest to them, still with no other purpose than the value they each derived from discussing issues and developments in the church.

As a result, I organized such meetings twice a year under the auspices of the center and under the very general title: consultations on pastoral priorities. There was a core of participants from the first gathering, and a few were added early on, but people attended as their calendars allowed. Cardinal Bernardin, for reasons we will note below, attended four of the meetings but kept in touch through his theological assistant, Father Michael Place, who was present for all the remaining sessions.

The conditions of the meeting were candor and confidentiality. The subjects at issue were the very ones that had given rise to the meetings—what was happening to the church's worship and religious education; the discussions going on about the Catholic identity of the church's health, education, and welfare institutions; the changing composition of ministry, with fewer priests and sisters and more lay persons and deacons; the church in the religious and secular media; alienation of youth; the roles of women in the church; and the place of Hispanic and African–American Catholics in the church. The agenda for each meeting was set at the prior meeting or in correspondence with participants in advance. Individual participants also agreed to prepare a subject in advance, circulate relevant articles, and initiate the conversation so that the discussion which was an end in itself might be as thoughtful as possible. I chaired the meetings.

Gradually members of the group came to think that their concerns and view of the situation might be more widely shared and that articulation of these concerns could be helpful to others who were feeling stymied in their pastoral efforts. The idea of a statement was proposed; it is lost to memory who first proposed it. The whole group discussed and agreed upon the basic content of the statement, various members of the group contributed sections, and gradually a statement was hammered out. This was not to be a manifesto that people would be called upon to sign or subscribe to. It was simply to be an appeal to the church, an invitation not only to reflect upon and discuss the condition of pastoral ministry as described in the statement, but also to consider whether the criteria for authentic and effective dialogue proposed in the statement spoke to individuals or groups in the church.

As the statement was being formulated, members of the group suggested that, besides issuing such an appeal, it would be useful to establish one response to it, an effort to conduct dialogue in the church that would both illumine a particular issue and identify methods and models of dialogue that could enhance discussion of issues in any forum.

This led to the idea of establishing the Catholic Common Ground Initiative. The Initiative would have a few modest purposes: conducting periodic conferences that would be an example of pursuing common ground and of constructive dialogue among people representing different perspectives and positions in the life of the church; occasional consultations that would assemble the best information about a subject so that those discussing it might be well informed in their discussions; occasional publications with the same approach and purposes; and an invitation to others in the church to consider the relevance of the statement and proposals for dialogue to their work.

CARDINAL BERNARDIN'S LEADERSHIP

I NOTED THAT the Initiative derives from a. process and a man. I need to say something about the man, Cardinal Bernardin. Cardinal Bernardin was at the heart of the gatherings of the pastoral consultation group from the beginning, even when he could not be present. The resulting statement and initiative reflect three basic qualities of Cardinal Bernardin: his thoroughgoing commitment to building up the community of the church, his attempt to reconcile people and viewpoints to the extent possible within the bounds of church teaching, and his appreciation for the wisdom and commitment of people throughout the church and beyond the church. His approach to leadership eminently exemplifies the basic stance and ecclesiology of the Pastoral Constitution on the Church in the Modern World of Vatican II and the words found in paragraph 92 of that document:

> In virtue of its mission to enlighten the whole world with the message of the Gospel and to gather together in one spirit all women and men of every nation, race, and culture, the church shows itself as a sign of that amity which renders possible sincere dialogue and strengthens it.
>
> Such a mission requires us first of all to create in the church itself mutual esteem, reverence, and harmony, and to acknowledge all legitimate diversity; in this way all who constitute the one people of God will be able to engage in ever more fruitful dialogue, whether they are pastors or other members of the faithful. For the ties which unite the faithful together are stronger than those which separate them: let there be unity in what is necessary, freedom in what is doubtful, and charity in everything.

Perhaps trust is at the heart of this approach, trust and the conviction that deep within our differences lies the unity we seek, the unity of Christ as way and truth and life. Trust, not naïveté. Trust in the Spirit, in the fruitfulness of respect and dialogue, trust that most other people are equally seeking integrity and the kind of humanity Christ exemplified. Trust in the church as the mystery of God's presence, the community of the Spirit, the best hope for humankind. Not naïveté regarding the presence of sin and darkness or the pride and self-centeredness that can distort dialogue. For dialogue must be grounded in both the teaching of the church and the best theological expertise one can assemble, and dialogue must be guided by a process that protects what is essential in the life of the church.

The statement and the Initiative both fit into the pattern of the Cardinal's life. And he rejected any separation between the two, as some critics implied, since he took part in creating both. Here was a man who devoted himself tirelessly to serving the unity among his fellow bishops in the National Conference of Catholic Bishops and through the triennial Synod of Bishops in Rome. He led the crafting of the historic pastoral letter of the American Catholic bishops on war and peace, "The Challenge of Peace: God's Promise and Our Response," with its precedent-setting consultation with the best of biblical and theological scholars, the most prominent leaders in military and diplomatic fields, and others—inside and outside the church—holding a broad range of viewpoints. His articulation of the consistent ethic of life offered a way within the bounds of church teaching of relating varied concerns about the sacredness and dignity of all human life and the varied groups and movements dedicated to one aspect or another of the threat to life.

But there is a personal side to the story, personal with enormous public dimensions. It was during the four years of gestation of the Initiative that Cardinal Bernardin suffered two profound afflictions, first, a charge of sexual abuse that was later withdrawn by the accuser, and then the onset of pancreatic cancer, which was to prove fateful. The way that he publicly confronted these two challenges to his life and integrity, and eventually death itself, lent a special credibility to his call to confront challenges to the life of the church. Furthermore, that he would continue to spend himself in what was hardly an obligatory involvement—the discussions and the founding of the Initiative—is at once a tribute to his determination to continue to give himself to his ministry and church whatever his personal travail and an indication of how serious he regarded the challenge faced by the church. He adverted to this in the press conference: "As I have said on several occasions, when one comes face to face with the reality of death in a very profound way as a cancer patient, one's perspective on life is altered dramatically. What seemed important before, now is seen as trivial, and what is truly important invites new commitment and a realignment of priorities." And, in his final public address on October 24, 1996, the first event of the Initiative: "A dying person does not have time for the peripheral or the accidental. He or she is drawn to the essential, the important—yes, the eternal. And what is important, my friends, is that we find that unity with the Lord and within the community of faith for which Jesus prayed so fervently on the night before he died."

This final public address was hastily organized because just two weeks after the announcement of the Initiative, Cardinal Bernardin learned that his cancer was no longer in remission and that he had very little time left. He died just some three weeks after the October 24 address.

THE MEANING OF COMMON GROUND

THOSE INVOLVED IN DRAFTING "Called to Be Catholic" struggled with the appropriate image for the goal they sought. The idea of trying to be "centrist" was discussed, centrist as contrasted with those who drift far to left or right.

But center suggests some single point. The single point is Jesus—and that was not at issue. As the statement confesses: "Jesus Christ, present in Scripture and sacrament, is central to all we do; he must always be the measure and not what is measured." Furthermore, what is centrist in common parlance depends very much on one's own perspective.

The Cardinal and the group became fixed on "common ground," with all its limitations. The meaning of common ground is best expressed where the statement avers that "Around this central conviction," namely, that Jesus Christ is central to all we do, "the church's leadership, both clerical and lay, must reaffirm and promote *the full range and demands of authentic unity, acceptable diversity, and respectful dialogue* [emphasis mine], not just as a way to dampen conflict but as a way to make our conflicts constructive, and ultimately as a way to understand for ourselves and articulate for our world the meaning of discipleship of Jesus." The origins of the dialogue lie in the mystery of the dialogue with the world that God entered into in the Incarnation of the Word, a mystery that continues to be expressed in the liturgy we celebrate. As Archbishop Oscar Lipscomb said in his keynote address to the first Initiative conference, "It is the *mysterium tremendum* encountered in the transforming experience of the church's public worship that provides our dialogue with its source and its goal." The goal is pastoral. The means involve an improved dialogue in the church, in which people representing diverse positions can honestly attend to the teaching of the church and the conditions of our time, while truly respecting one another, listening to one another. In such a dialogue, we all might find where attention to the faith we share leads to common ground in the efforts we make. The whole church might even benefit from achieving what, in his widely quoted statement, John Courtney Murray called "genuine disagreement."

The pursuit of common ground, a pastoral project, requires recognition that the church as a mysterious communion is not to be reduced to the negotiating of contrary opinions, and must operate with the bounds of, and be accountable to, both the tradition of the church and the living magisterium exercised by the bishops and the Chair of Peter. It also requires a way of engaging one another and the tradition that observes basic principles of respectful dialogue which, as some have observed, is ultimately a spirituality.

AFTERMATH OF THE ANNOUNCEMENT

THE ANNOUNCEMENT OF the Initiative and publication of the statement elicited widespread and strongly expressed reactions, most of which were enthusiastically supportive, some of which were equally critical. Many letters, articles, editorials and phone calls expressed support for the Initiative and heartfelt agreement that the statement well described the situation of the Catholic Church in the United States. Pastors wrote that the entire enterprise addressed concerns they had but which they felt were not being attended to by church leadership. Individual parishioners also wrote that the statement reflected both disagreements they found in their own parishes or parish councils, and the situation in the church that they felt was sapping energy from the church's basic mission.

PROFESSORS OF THEOLOGY and others in Catholic colleges and universities, themselves still engaged in discussions of the Catholic identity of their institutions, found the effort quite relevant and complementary to their own discussions. Many of them, professors and college presidents, offered the services of their departments and institutions for furthering the goals of the Initiative. They could sponsor forums that would address the issues that had been raised and do so specifically within the common ground framework, that is, bringing together representatives of different viewpoints so that they could engage one another's arguments and clarify both unacknowledged agreement and where true disagreement lay. One moral theology professor wrote that the statement had a profound impact on him, leading him to reflect on how well he presents the views of those with whom he disagrees.

Not all those supporting the effort pointed to polarization as their concern. What was common to all, however, was the expectation that the Initiative might help promote better discussion in the church. The word "hope" was expressed in many letters, implied in most—hope that a new spirit of honest dialogue might replace what seemed at a stalemate, caused by a refusal to discuss difficult issues.

Many writers indicated that they are going ahead on their own, as Cardinal Bernardin had hoped, undertaking initiatives in their own parishes, schools, universities, or other church forums. Other writers recommended books, institutes, and particular resources for dialogue.

The critical reactions came not only from the four cardinals, but from writers, editors, and activists of varying perspectives. Some of the critics worried that too open a dialogue might, within the current liberal culture, suggest that everything is open to question and negotiation, every participant of equal authority, and any consensus, however reached, of equal value, thereby undermining both church teaching and the teaching authority of the church. Concern about widespread "relativism" regarding basic truths of the church lay behind much of this critique. Among these were voices expressing the view that what is most needed is clearer presentation of official church teaching and greater readiness to accept and adhere to that teaching. Still others felt that the statement gave insufficient attention to the essentially spiritual task of engaging the message of Christ and teaching of the church and the conversion away from sin and toward Christ that is a necessary condition for true dialogue.

Criticism of quite a different stripe opposed the very idea of "the boundaries of Catholic Christianity" which the statement indicates as the necessary context of dialogue. Implying that there is no clear authority for establishing such boundaries, this criticism suggested that the dialogue would be flawed without accepting as partners all those who claim Catholic identity whatever their convictions or positions. Still another criticism argued that polarization is a problem among the elites of the church, but is not a major factor among most members of the church (in fact, the statement itself locates polarization particularly in relation to "leaders, both clerical and lay"). Another was that the statement omitted certain factors in church life that were claimed to be most responsible for the polarization in the church.

Cardinal Bernardin addressed many of these criticisms in a statement, drafted in question-and-answer format, which he released on August 29, 1996. In that statement, he identified three main criticisms: "First, that it does not adequately acknowledge Scripture and tradition as the actual common ground of the Catholic Church and reduces the magisterium to just one voice in a chorus of debate. Second, that it places dissent on the same level as truth and seems ready to accept compromise of the truth. Third, that it insufficiently acknowledges the centrality of Jesus." His response to each of these criticisms and other questions can be found in the release on page 49.

Many have observed that the reactions to the statement confirm the very condition described in it, namely, a polarizing tendency that leads from disagreement to warnings that an enterprise threatens the unity and teaching of the church. Others have observed that certain reactions make clear that relativism—the stance that positions sincerely held are self-validating and need not meet the test of the tradition nor be accountable to the teaching office of the church—is a real danger among Catholics. The criticisms also had the effect of helping to clarify both the terms of the analysis in the statement, "Called to Be Catholic" and the intent of the Initiative.

ORGANIZATION AND ACTIVITY OF THE INITIATIVE

WHEN CARDINAL BERNARDIN decided to establish the Initiative and serve as its leader, it became clear that he needed the assistance of a group of people specifically chosen to further the Initiative. This formal group had to be more carefully chosen than were the participants in the original consultations. For this purpose, he assembled a Cardinal's Committee for the Catholic Common Ground Initiative, composed of twenty-five people representing a broad range of positions and perspectives in the church. (The members are listed at the end of this introduction.) He invited about half of those who had been part of the original discussion group to continue, and in order to achieve a greater diversity of views and positions in the church he invited others to join. Those who had taken part in all or some of the earlier discussion understood

the need to reorganize. Even as the Cardina
with those who were able to accept his invitatic
group, he realized that the group was not full}
tive, a defect that would have to be addressed once the Initiative was underway.

His invitation asked that the person basically accept the
statement "Called to Be Catholic" as a starting point for the
effort without necessarily agreeing with every aspect of the
statement. Individuals could and did demur from some
aspects and would have made other changes. But they were
not asked to sign the statement—it was neither a manifesto,
nor a final word, simply an expression of concern and a call
to action.

When his death became imminent, Cardinal Bernardin
asked Archbishop Oscar Lipscomb of Mobile, Alabama, to
succeed him as chair. The Archbishop agreed to do so. Archbishop Lipscomb, a native of Alabama with a doctorate in
church history, has served on committees of the National
Conference of Catholic Bishops that provide rich back-
ground for the work of the Initiative. He served a term as
chair of the committee on doctrine, guiding the consultation and voting process for the conference statement on the
relationship between the magisterium (teaching authority of
the church) and theologians. His experience would serve the
Initiative well in achieving the right balance between accep-
tance of church teaching and openness to greater understanding of faith and discipleship. He has also chaired the
conference committee engaged in the dialogue between the
Roman Catholic Church and the Orthodox Church. Much
of the developing understanding of the meaning and methods of authentic dialogue has come through the ecumenical
movement. This experience will have much to offer our

efforts at intrachurch dialogue. The Archbishop's reply to Cardinal Bernardin's original invitation to serve on the committee itself reflected well the kind of tolerance of differences that the Initiative hopes to encourage. For, regarding the statement, "Called to Be Catholic," he wrote that he agreed with about ninety percent of it, which is more than he did with many other statements. In other words, he did not have to agree with a hundred percent in order to find sufficient common ground for joining the effort.

The full committee met for the first time with Cardinal Bernardin on October 24. At this meeting it set forth basic directions for the Initiative and determined to go ahead with the first conference in March 1997. The National Pastoral Life Center, which had worked with Cardinal Bernardin from the beginning, would continue to serve as the secretariat for the Initiative.

Between the announcement and the first committee meeting, however, widespread enthusiasm had greeted the Initiative in many quarters. Cardinal Bernardin had sent the statement to a number of church organizations, inviting them to consider its relevance for their work, and had received very encouraging replies from many. Many people in parishes, dioceses, colleges and universities, national church organizations, and other groups expressed a desire not only to support the Initiative but to participate in the pursuit of common ground. Because of this response, the committee agreed that the Initiative had to go beyond the original modest plans for action. The Initiative had to serve this widespread interest with suggestions, resource materials, guidelines, and other aides both to support independent efforts and to spread the responsibility for pursuing the goal. The committee charged the secretariat with developing these resources.

THE INITIATIVE

THE INAUGURAL CONFERENCE of the Catholic Common Ground Initiative on the theme "The U.S. Culture and the Challenge of Discipleship" was held at Mundelein Seminary outside Chicago March 7–9. On May 10, the Initiative conducted an interactive teleconference over Odyssey, the ecumenical cable television network, on the same theme, involving a wider audience in the discussion.

Assembled at the conference were forty people, eighteen committee members and twenty-two others, reflecting a variety of positions in the church and perspectives on church issues. The intent was to have a group large enough to include the diverse viewpoints the Initiative intends to bring together, but small enough that there could be real dialogue among the participants. Other than the opening session, the conference was closed to the public and the media in order to encourage people to speak freely and candidly, expressing opinions they might not want to be held accountable for without further consideration, and challenging one another in ways they might not do in a public meeting. Archbishop Lipscomb opened the conference with an address entitled "Dialogue: A Labor in Love." In that presentation, he both further clarified the purpose of the Initiative and specifically addressed criticisms that had been published since the death of Cardinal Bernardin, primarily regarding the conditions for authentic dialogue. The text appears on page 79.

The conference continued during the two days that followed with discussion of the topic. The discussion reflected the variety of backgrounds, concerns, and perspectives of the participants: the more academic and the more directly pastoral, those from different ethnic and cultural backgrounds, those whose experience is mostly local and those whose reflections are national or global, those whose contributions to the church are mostly in the areas of theology or worship and those who concentrate on the church's social ministry.

Prior to the conference, the committee met for the first time under Archbishop Lipscomb's leadership. This was a critical transition point, moving from the individual members' commitment in response to Cardinal Bernardin's personal invitation to join him in the Initiative toward the commitment of the group to take responsibility for the Initiative. The committee charged the secretariat to move ahead with the original plans and to find ways to respond to the widespread desire to work in tandem with the Initiative.

The Initiative will, consequently, conduct conferences like the first one at least yearly. The secretariat has also begun to publish a newsletter that contains reports of Initiative activity, suggestions regarding methods of dialogue, reports of other "common ground" efforts throughout the church, and resources. The Initiative is producing an initial guide for parish activities and will publish a variety of other materials focusing on various topics for dialogue, on the conduct of dialogue, and on the approaches to dialogue that are appropriate to educational and pastoral institutions in the church.

The papers in this volume are the founding documents. They are that but only that. In publishing them, the Initiative hopes to make available exactly what Cardinal Bernardin and the founders intended. The committee hopes that all who are inspired by the Initiative, either to support it or to criticize it, will take the time to read these papers and consider them respectfully as the documents speak to their own experience and understanding of the life of the church. Are the issues identified in the statement the critical issues? Which are not so critical? What issues are missing? Are there more basic issues that lie beneath these and other challenges facing the church? Is the condition of discussion and dialogue in one's situation as it is described in the statement and further elaborated on in Cardinal Bernardin's and Archbishop Lipscomb's addresses? Is the call to dialogue needed and, if so, with what conditions for authentic dialogue—those that are described in Cardinal Bernardin's October 24 address, Archbishop Lipscomb's address on dialogue, and in the "Called to Be Catholic" statement? Are the working principles described at the end of the statement principles to which one would subscribe? Are these principles regularly observed in one's own efforts? And if not, should they be observed more faithfully or are they inappropriate in certain situations? Are there other working principles that would enhance dialogue within the church? What will it take to make the engagement in dialogue an expression of truly and specifically Catholic spirituality?

These are only founding documents. The experiences and expressions of new efforts at dialogue sponsored by the Catholic Common Ground Initiative and undertaken by others, to say nothing of further documents from the teaching office of the church, will surely take us further along in breaking and clearing new ground upon which to carry on the pastoral mission of the church.

COMMITTEE FOR THE CATHOLIC COMMON GROUND INITIATIVE

Most Rev. Oscar H.
Lipscomb, *Chair*
Archbishop of Mobile, AL

Hon. Robert B. Casey
Scranton, PA

Rev. Brian Daley, S.J.
University of Notre Dame, IN

*Mr. Thomas Donnelly
Houston, Donnelly & Meck
Pittsburgh, PA

Rev. Virgilio Elizondo
Mexican-American Cultural
Center
San Antonio, TX

Dr. Mary Ann Glendon
Harvard Law School
Cambridge, MA

*Sr. Doris Gottemoeller,
R.S.M.
President, Sisters of Mercy
Silver Spring, MD

*Rev. J. Bryan Hehir
Center for International Affairs
Harvard University
Cambridge, MA

*Rev. Robert Imbelli
Boston College
Newton, MA

Sr. Elizabeth Johnson, C.S.J.
Fordham University
Bronx, NY

Cardinal Roger Mahony
Archbishop of Los Angeles, CA

*Most Rev. James W. Malone
Bishop Emeritus
Youngstown, OH

*Rev. Msgr. Philip J. Murnion
National Pastoral Life Center
New York, NY

Hon. John T. Noonan, Jr.
U.S. Circuit Court Judge
Berkeley, CA

THE DOCUMENTS

1. CALLED TO BE CATHOLIC:
CHURCH IN A TIME OF PERIL

This statement was released by Cardinal Bernardin on August 12, 1996, on the occasion of the announcement of the Catholic Common Ground Initiative. It was prepared by the National Pastoral Life Center as the result of a series of consultations involving Cardinal Bernardin and a group of bishops, priests, religious, and lay people.

2. THE CATHOLIC COMMON GROUND
NEWS CONFERENCE

This was the prepared statement delivered by Cardinal Bernardin at the news conference announcing the Initiative at the offices of the Archdiocese of Chicago on August 12, 1996.

3. QUESTIONS AND ANSWERS REGARDING
THE CATHOLIC COMMON GROUND PROJECT

This set of questions and answers was sent to all the Catholic bishops of the United States by Cardinal Bernardin on August 29, 1996, and released to the media on August 30, to answer questions that had arisen regarding the Initiative and the statement, "Called to Be Catholic."

4. FAITHFUL AND HOPEFUL: THE CATHOLIC COMMON GROUND PROJECT

This is the text of the last formal address of Cardinal Bernardin before he died. The occasion was the first meeting of the Committee for the Catholic Common Ground Initiative and the first public conference in Chicago on October 24, 1996.

5. DIALOGUE: A LABOR IN LOVE

Archbishop Oscar H. Lipscomb delivered this address at the opening of the first Cardinal Bernardin Conference of the Initiative in Mundelein, Illinois, on March 7, 1997.

1

CALLED TO BE CATHOLIC: CHURCH IN A TIME OF PERIL

Inaugural Statement of the
Catholic Common Ground Project

CALLED TO BE CATHOLIC *was prepared by the National Pastoral Life Center in consultation with Catholic men and women serving the church and society in a variety of callings and sensitive to the diversity of Catholicism in the United States.*

This statement provides the basis for the Catholic Common Ground Project. The project will sponsor conferences and papers devoted to critical issues in the church and will exemplify and promote the kind of dialogue called for in this statement.

All organizations and groups in the church are invited to consider the CALLED TO BE CATHOLIC *statement and its applications to their meetings, conferences, and deliberations. Responses to the statement are welcome and may be sent to the National Pastoral Life Center, 18 Bleecker Street, New York, N.Y. 10012.*

I

Will the Catholic Church in the United States enter the new millennium as a church of promise, augmented by the faith of rising generations and able to be a leavening force in our culture? Or will it become a church on the defensive, torn by dissension and weakened in its core structures? The outcome, we believe, depends on whether American Catholicism can confront an array of challenges with honesty and imagination and whether the church can reverse the polarization that inhibits discussion and cripples leadership. American Catholics must reconstitute the conditions for addressing our differences constructively— a common ground centered on faith in Jesus, marked by accountability to the living Catholic tradition, and ruled by a renewed spirit of civility, dialogue, generosity, and broad and serious consultation.

It is widely admitted that the Catholic Church in the United States has entered a time of peril. Many of its leaders, both clerical and lay, feel under siege and increasingly polarized. Many of its faithful, particularly its young people, feel disenfranchised, confused about their beliefs, and increasingly adrift. Many of its institutions feel uncertain of their identity and increasingly fearful about their future.

Those are hard words to pronounce to a church that, despite many obstacles, continues to grow in numbers, continues to welcome and assist the poor and the stranger, and continues to foster extraordinary examples of Christian faith and witness to the gospel. The landscape of American Catholicism is dotted with vital communities of worship and service, with new initiatives, and with older, deeply rooted endeavors that are kept alive by the hard labor and daily sacrifices of millions of Catholics. In the face of powerful centrifugal forces, many Catholic leaders have worked to build consensus and cooperation.

We hesitate to say anything that might discourage them or add to the fingerpointing and demoralization that, in too many cases, already burden these exemplary efforts. But this discordant and disheartened atmosphere is itself one of the realities which cannot be ignored. For three decades the church has been divided by different responses to the Second Vatican Council and to the tumultuous years that followed it. By no means were these tensions always unfruitful; in many cases they were virtually unavoidable.

But even as conditions have changed, party lines have hardened. A mood of suspicion and acrimony hangs over many of those most active in the church's life; at moments it even seems to have infiltrated the ranks of the bishops. One consequence is that many of us are refusing to acknowledge disquieting realities, perhaps fearing that they may reflect poorly on our past efforts or arm our critics within the church. Candid discussion is inhibited. Across the whole spectrum of views within the church, proposals are subject to ideological litmus tests. Ideas, journals, and leaders are pressed to align themselves with preexisting camps, and are viewed warily when they depart from those expectations.

There is nothing wrong in itself with the prospect that different visions should contend within American Catholicism. That has long been part of the church's experience in this nation, and indeed differences of opinion are essential to the process of attaining the truth. But the way that struggle is currently proceeding, the entire church may lose. It is now three decades after Vatican II. Social and cultural circumstances have changed. The church possesses a wealth of postconciliar experience to assess and translate into lessons for the future. There is undiminished hunger for authentic faith, spiritual experience, and moral guidance, but many of the traditional supports for distinct religious identities—or for the institutions that convey them—have disappeared.

Meanwhile, positions of leadership in the ministries of the church are passing to those with little exposure, for better or worse, to the sharply defined institutional Catholicism of earlier decades. Still younger Catholics, many with absolutely no experience of that preconciliar Catholicism, come to the church with new questions and few of the old answers.

The church's capacity to respond to these changed conditions may be stymied if constructive debate is supplanted by bickering, disparagement, and stalemate. Rather than forging a consensus that can harness and direct the church's energies, contending viewpoints are in danger of canceling one another out. Bishops risk being perceived as members of different camps rather than as pastors of the whole church.

Unless we examine our situation with fresh eyes, open minds and changed hearts, within a few decades a vital Catholic legacy may be squandered, to the loss of both the church and the nation.

II

THERE ARE URGENT questions that the church in the United States knows it must air openly and honestly, but which it increasingly feels pressed to evade or, at best, address obliquely. These issues include:

- the changing roles of women;
- the organization and effectiveness of religious education;
- the Eucharistic liturgy as most Catholics experience it;
- the meaning of human sexuality, and the gap between church teachings and the convictions of many faithful in this and several other areas of morality;
- the image and morale of priests, and the declining ratios of priests and vowed religious to people in the pews;
- the succession of lay people to positions of leadership formerly held by priests and sisters, and the provision of an adequate formation for ministers, both ordained and lay;
- the ways in which the church is present in political life, its responsibility to the poor and defenseless, and its support for lay people in their family life and daily callings;
- the capacity of the church to embrace African–American, Latino, and Asian populations, their cultural heritages and their social concerns;
- the survival of Catholic school systems, colleges and universities, health care facilities and social services,

and the articulation of a distinct and appropriate religious identity and mission for these institutions;
- the dwindling financial support from parishioners;
- the manner of decision-making and consultation in church governance;
- the responsibility of theology to authoritative church teachings;
- the place of collegiality and subsidiarity in the relations between Rome and the American episcopacy.

As long as such topics remain inadequately addressed, the near future of American Catholic life is at risk. Yet in almost every case, the necessary conversation runs up against polarized positions that have so magnified fears and so strained sensitivities that even the simplest lines of inquiry are often fiercely resisted. Consider, for example, just two of these topics.

On every side, there are reports that many Catholics are reaching adulthood with barely a rudimentary knowledge of their faith, with an attenuated sense of sacrament, and with a highly individualistic view of the church. Some of us are tempted to minimize the seriousness of this situation out of an attachment to young people and an appreciation of their generosity—or out of loyalty to those who work, often with insufficient resources and scant rewards, to provide religious education. Others among us rush to reduce complex questions of pedagogy, theology, limited time, turnover in teachers, and the pressures of an aggressive and pervasive youth culture to some single factor—and some simple solution.

The practical realities of our young people's needs are quickly lost amid accusations of infidelity to church teachings, reflexive defenses against criticism, or promotion of pet educational approaches. It is an atmosphere unlikely to generate the massive and creative effort required to meet today's crisis of religious illiteracy or link it with young people's search for a sense of participation and belonging.

Or consider the church's public prayer. The faith thrives where the Eucharist is celebrated worthily, drawing the Christian community into its mystery and power. Yet in many parishes Mass attendance has plummeted; congregational participation is indifferent; and liturgies are marred by lack of preparation, casual or rushed gestures, unsuitable music, and banal sentiments in hymns and, above all, in homilies. There is widespread awareness that, thirty years after the council, the goals of liturgical renewal have been met more in letter than in spirit.

But again polarization blocks a candid and constructive response to the situation. An informal or "horizontal" liturgy, demystified and stressing the participation of the congregation, is pitted against a solemn or "vertical" liturgy, unchangeable and focused on the sacerdotal action of the priest. The former is rightly feared as unable to carry the weight of the transcendent, and as opening the liturgy to the trivializing currents of the culture. The latter is rightly feared as becoming a concert, a show, or a spiritless exercise in rubrics, closed to the particular needs and gifts of the community. No effort to assess the state of worship or develop new translations or refresh liturgical skills escapes suspicion of moving to one extreme or the other—or pressure to move in the opposite direction as a safeguard.

The same dynamic of fear and polarization afflicts the church's discussions of other topics, from efforts to accommodate language or practice to the changing consciousness of women to efforts to define theology's relationship to the hierarchy. Unnuanced positions are espoused without encountering moderating criticism from sympathizers. Then these positions loom even more powerfully as fears in the minds of opponents, generating or justifying their own unnuanced positions. The end results are distrust, acrimony, and deadlock.

III

WHAT WILL IT TAKE for the Catholic Church in the United States to escape from this partisanship and the paralysis it threatens to engender?

Jesus Christ, present in Scripture and sacrament, is central to all that we do; he must always be the measure and not what is measured.

Around this central conviction, the church's leadership, both clerical and lay, must reaffirm and promote the full range and demands of authentic unity, acceptable diversity, and respectful dialogue, not just as a way to dampen conflict but as a way to make our conflicts constructive, and ultimately as a way to understand for ourselves and articulate for our world the meaning of discipleship of Jesus Christ.

This invitation to a revitalized Catholic common ground should not be limited to those who agree in every respect on an orientation for the church, but encompass all—whether centrists, moderates, liberals, radicals, conservatives, or neoconservatives—who are willing to reaffirm basic truths and to pursue their disagreements in a renewed spirit of dialogue.

Chief among those truths is that our discussion must be accountable to the Catholic tradition and to the Spirit-filled, living church that brings to us the revelation of God in

Jesus. To say this does not resolve a host of familiar questions about the way that the church has preserved, interpreted, and communicated that revelation. Accountability to the Catholic tradition does not mean reversion to a chain-of-command, highly institutional understanding of the church, a model resembling a modern corporation, with headquarters and branch offices, rather than Vatican II's vision of a communion and a people.

Nor does accountability mean conceiving of faith as an ideology, an all-encompassing doctrinal system that produces ready explanations and practical prescriptions for every human question. Now, as historically, there has always been wide room for legitimate debate, discussion, and diversity. But accountability does demand serious engagement with the tradition and its authoritative representatives. It rules out the pop scholarship, sound-bite theology, unhistorical assertions, and flippant dismissals that have become all too common on both the right and the left of the church. Authentic accountability rules out a fundamentalism that narrows the richness of the tradition to a text or a decree, and it rules out a narrow appeal to individual or contemporary experience that ignores the cloud of witnesses over the centuries or the living magisterium of the church exercised by the bishops and the Chair of Peter.

Authentic accountability embraces the demands that the gospel poses for our public life and social structures as well as for our private lives and personal relations. This accountability implies that the church, for all its humanness, cannot be treated as merely a human organization. The church is a chosen people, a mysterious communion, a foreshadowing of the Kingdom, a spiritual family. One implication of this is that the hermeneutic of suspicion must be balanced with a hermeneutic of love and retrieval. Another is that an essential element of Catholic leadership must be wide and serious consultation, especially of those most affected by church policies under examination. The church's ancient concept of reception reminds us that all the faithful are called to a role in grasping a truth or incorporating a decision or practice into the church's life.

Finally this accountability recognizes that our discussions about the Catholic Church take place within boundaries. Exactly how the boundaries of Catholic Christianity should be formulated will inevitably be open at times to reexamination and debate. So too will our attitudes toward whatever falls outside those boundaries. But the very idea of boundaries is a necessary premise, without which no identity can exist. Inclusivity, a concept that can operate at many levels, becomes a catchword and even a self-contradiction when it impugns any efforts to make distinctions or set defining limits.

IV

THE REVITALIZED CATHOLIC common ground, we suggested, will be marked by a willingness to approach the church's current situation with fresh eyes, open minds, and changed hearts. It will mean pursuing disagreements in a renewed spirit of dialogue. Specifically, we urge that Catholics be guided by working principles like these:

- We should recognize that no single group or viewpoint in the church has a complete monopoly on the truth. While the bishops united with the Pope have been specially endowed by God with the power to preserve the true faith, they too exercise their office by taking counsel with one another and with the experience of the whole church, past and present. Solutions to the church's problems will almost inevitably emerge from a variety of sources.

- We should not envision ourselves or any one part of the church a saving remnant. No group within the church should judge itself alone to be possessed of enlightenment or spurn the mass of Catholics, their leaders, or their institutions as unfaithful.

- We should test all proposals for their pastoral realism and potential impact on living individuals as well as for their theological truth. Pastoral effectiveness is a responsibility of leadership.

- We should presume that those with whom we differ are acting in good faith. They deserve civility, charity, and a good-faith effort to understand their concerns. We should not substitute labels, abstractions, or blanketing terms—"radical feminism," "the hierarchy," "the Vatican"—for living, complicated realities.

- We should put the best possible construction on differing positions, addressing their strongest points rather than seizing upon the most vulnerable aspects in order to discredit them. We should detect the valid insights and legitimate worries that may underlie even questionable arguments.

- We should be cautious in ascribing motives. We should not impugn another's love of the church and loyalty to it. We should not rush to interpret disagreements as conflicts of starkly opposing principles rather than as differences in degree or in prudential pastoral judgments about the relevant facts.

- We should bring the church to engage the realities of contemporary culture, not by simple defiance or by naïve acquiescence, but acknowledging, in the fashion of *Gaudium et Spes*, both our culture's valid achievements and real dangers.

Ultimately, the fresh eyes and changed hearts we need cannot be distilled from guidelines. They emerge in the space created by praise and worship. The revitalized Catholic common ground will be marked by a determined pastoral effort to keep the liturgy, above all, from becoming a battleground for confrontation and polarization, and to treasure it as the common worship of God through Jesus Christ in the communion of the Holy Spirit.

IT IS IMPERATIVE that the Catholic Church in the United States confront the issues and forces that are shaping the future. For this, we must draw on all the gifts of wisdom and understanding in the church, all the charisms of leadership and communion. Each of us will be tested by encounters with cultures and viewpoints not our own; all of us will be refined in the fires of genuine engagement; and the whole church will be strengthened for its mission in the new millennium.

[This statement was prepared by the National Pastoral Life Center, Rev. Msgr. Philip J. Murnion, Director.]

2

THE CATHOLIC COMMON GROUND NEWS CONFERENCE

Remarks by Joseph Cardinal Bernardin
August 12, 1996

Thank you for coming today! I am very grateful that Mr. Thomas Donnelly, Sister Doris Gottemoeller, Monsignor Philip Murnion, and Professor James Kelly (Secretary) are with me as I announce this new endeavor.

As many of you know, I have been a Roman Catholic bishop for over thirty years. My episcopal service began shortly after the Second Vatican Council ended. In large measure my pastoral ministry has been concerned with implementing the teaching and pastoral directives of that ecumenical council, which, I believe, was truly the work of God's Holy Spirit.

In carrying out my pastoral responsibilities, I have been sustained by the example of two great churchmen who served as my mentors: John Cardinal Dearden of Detroit and Archbishop Paul Hallinan of Atlanta. I learned a great deal from them—for example, to trust that, through open and honest dialogue, differences can be resolved and the integrity of the gospel proclaimed. I have tried to do this throughout my ministry as Archbishop of Cincinnati and, now, of Chicago; as general secretary and, later, as president of the National Conference of Catholic Bishops (NCCB), as chairperson of several NCCB committees, and in recent years as senior active Cardinal in the United States.

More recently, however, I have been troubled that an increasing polarization within the church and, at times, a meanspiritedness have hindered the kind of dialogue that helps us address our mission and concerns. As a result, the unity of the church is threatened, the great gift of the Second Vatican Council is in danger of being seriously undermined, the faithful members of the church are weary, and our witness to government, society, and culture is compromised.

While these are not new realities, in the past year I have come to see them in a new light. As I have said on several occasions, when one comes face to face with the reality of death in a very profound way as a cancer patient, one's perspective on life is altered dramatically. What seemed so important before, now is seen as trivial, and what is truly important invites new commitment and a realignment of priorities.

It is in this context that I am pleased to announce today the inauguration of what is being called the Catholic Common

Ground Project. This endeavor is inspired by a statement I am making public today, a statement that emerged from a series of discussions in which I participated. These discussions began more than three years ago. The paper is entitled "Called to Be Catholic: Church in a Time of Peril." It decries the growing polarization in the church, which hinders our addressing important pastoral concerns, and calls for a new kind of dialogue that will engage people of diverse viewpoints in the church. I am releasing this statement today with the invitation and the hope that other Catholic individuals and groups will study it carefully and consider its implications for the way in which they carry out their responsibilities in church life.

The Catholic Common Ground Project that the committee and I are undertaking is one response to this statement. Using the teaching of the Second Vatican Council as its basis for dialogue, this Project will sponsor conferences that bring together persons of diverse perspectives in search of a "Catholic common ground." Working within the boundaries of authentic church teaching, these conferences will address with fidelity and creativity the myriad challenges that we face as a church and as a society. With this approach we should find ways to enhance our common worship, our religious education efforts, and our outreach to those in need. Our tentative plans call for a conference in early 1997 on the relationship between the church and U.S. culture, developed in the context of the Pastoral Constitution on the church in the Modern World of Vatican II (*Gaudium et Spes*). The conference will address such questions as: In what ways can we bring the gospel to bear on our culture? In what ways are we positively or negatively affected by our culture?

I am very grateful that seven bishops and sixteen other prominent Catholic leaders have agreed to join me in overseeing the Project's initiatives. The diversity among my colleagues demonstrates that there is a desire in all parts of the church to pursue the goals of this Project.

I am also very grateful to Monsignor Philip Murnion and the National Pastoral Life Center for agreeing to serve as staff for the Project. I look forward to working with Professor James Kelly, who will serve as secretary of the Project. Father Michael Place will serve as my liaison to the Project.

Let me conclude by speaking directly to my sisters and brothers in the Lord here in Chicago and throughout this great land:

> Our faith and our common life as members of the community of faith, which is the church, are indeed great and precious gifts. Let us together leave behind whatever brings discord. Let us recommit ourselves to our great heritage of faith. Let us walk in communion with, and in loyalty to, our Holy Father in order to restore and strengthen the unity that has been fractured or diminished. And may our service to the Lord God and to our world be enhanced by our efforts to reclaim the "Catholic common ground" that can support renewed and revitalized lives of faith as we enter the third millennium of Christianity.

3

QUESTIONS AND ANSWERS
REGARDING THE CATHOLIC
COMMON GROUND PROJECT

Press Statement by Joseph Cardinal
Bernardin, August 29, 1996

On August 12, I announced an initiative aimed at getting beyond the entrenched positions and polarization that I believe are blocking critically needed fresh thinking about the challenges facing the Catholic Church in the United States. There have been many strong reactions to the announcement of the formation of the Catholic Common Ground Project, much of it very favorable, some of it decidedly critical. I thought it would be helpful to respond, with gratitude, to the positive reactions and address in greater detail the issues that seem to be the cause of several of the principal criticisms. A question/answer format seems best suited for this purpose.

Why did you hold the August 12 press conference?

First, to release a statement I was involved in developing: "Called to Be Catholic: Church in a Time of Peril." The statement identifies some of the pastoral issues we need to address and calls for a new kind of discussion. Second, as one response to this call, I announced the formation of the Catholic Common Ground Project.

What positive reactions have you received?

We have received calls and letters from bishops, parishioners, pastors, women and men religious, professors, and individuals working in diocesan offices. With rare exceptions, they thanked us for spelling out fears and hopes about the church that they have long entertained. Furthermore, many of them wanted to know what they can do in their own communities. I was particularly gratified by the support of Bishop Anthony Pilla, president of the National Conference of Catholic Bishops.

What are the criticisms?

Some of these have been sharp indeed. To some extent, they confirm the need for this initiative. Even a carefully framed appeal for dialogue coming from an archbishop and seconded by a broad range of distinguished advisors was met with immediate suspicion.

Of course, we anticipated criticisms from some groups on the right or left who are convinced that anything not explicitly committed to their respective agenda will only strengthen their adversaries or legitimate the status quo. They simply do not see the situation as we do.

More troubling is the criticism that mixes arguable points with what I believe are grave misunderstandings.

A lot of criticism focused on the statement, "Called to Be Catholic." Let's start with that. What is its origin?

About four years ago, I had a conversation about parish life with Monsignor Philip Murnion of the National Pastoral Life Center. We discussed how conflicts between certain camps in the church were hindering efforts to address serious pastoral challenges. It occurred to us that further discussion of this problem might be helpful. Over the ensuing years, the center held a number of consultations with clergy, religious, and laity in a variety of positions in the church. I participated in a number of these discussions. Some of us thought that a statement describing the situation and calling for pastoral discussion, which would take into account a variety of perspectives, might encourage others. The statement was developed by the center from the contributions of a number of people. I was in touch with this effort, and in no way do I wish to be distanced from the statement.

What, then, is the advisory committee's relationship to the statement?

First, it was not our intention to ask anyone to sign the statement; that would have given it too much importance and suggested that it must be accepted in its entirety. When I decided that an effort should be made to foster the kind of dialogue called for by the statement, I felt the need for an advisory committee that would represent diverse positions and responsibilities in the church. In inviting people to serve on this committee, I asked if they could accept the statement as a good starting point for the effort, even if not every phrase or point was to their liking. This is what they agreed to. Perhaps the best way of describing their relationship is Archbishop Oscar Lipscomb's reply that he could accept about ninety percent of the statement, which is better than usual in the present environment within the church.

What are the main criticisms of the statement, and how do you respond to them?

As I see it, three major criticism have been made about the statement. First, that it does not adequately acknowledge Scripture and tradition as the actual common ground of the Catholic Church and reduces the magisterium to just one more voice in a chorus of debate. Second, that it places dissent on the same level as truth and seems ready to accept compromise of the truth. Third, that it insufficiently acknowledges the centrality of Jesus.

My response to the first criticism is that Scripture and tradition are the foundational sources of church teaching and, therefore, the basis for the "common ground." The primacy of Scripture and tradition is fully recognized in the statement. The statement also clearly calls for accountability to the Catholic tradition and rejects any approach that would ignore the "living magisterium of the church exercised by the bishops and the chair of Peter."

In regard to the second criticism, the statement's call to dialogue within the church no more legitimates dissent than does dialogue with other faith traditions. In fact, the question of dissent in the church and whether it is ever justified is a complicated and theologically technical one, and our statement did not pursue it.

The premise of our statement is that many serious disagreements among Catholics—for example, about the state of the liturgy or religious education or the role of women in the church—do not necessarily involve dissent in the sense of a clear departure from authentic teaching. But the statement also shows full awareness that such departures do exist. The statement recognizes the legitimacy, even the value, of disagreements, but it also insists that dialogue about them must be accountable to Catholic tradition and the church's teaching authority. Likewise, the statement insists that "discussion about the Catholic Church take place within boundaries" and "defining limits." It explicitly challenges two of the most popular reasons for dismissing tradition or boundaries, the appeals to "experience" and to "inclusivity."

In a few paragraphs the statement tries to capture both the demands and the dynamism of orthodoxy. It is willing to consider the new but insists that it be accountable to tradition and the magisterium. This clearly is not establishing truth by compromise or accommodation.

In regard to the third criticism, the statement begins by asserting that the very first condition for addressing our differences constructively must be "a common ground centered on faith in Jesus." Moreover, in the statement's section proposing a solution it again begins with the profession: "Jesus Christ, present in Scripture and sacrament, is central to all we do. He must always be the measure and not what is measured."

I am convinced that a careful reading of the text ought to reassure those who expressed these concerns.

But hasn't the very idea of dialogue become questionable? Isn't it a slogan to elude or erode church teaching or to prevent closure on a subject? Is it sufficient to resolve all issues?

There are some legitimate fears in this area. Yes, the idea of dialogue has sometimes been cheapened by turning it into a tool of single-minded advocacy. It is also true that dialogue is not in every case or at every moment the universal solution to all conflicts.

Nevertheless, I am convinced that, in the United States today, dialogue is a critical need. The church is built up, not brought down, by genuine dialogue anchored in our fundamental teachings. While millions of Catholics of good will cannot deny their concerns and dissatisfactions, they do not want to be drawn into some basically hostile posture toward the church and its teaching. It is essential that we offer these faithful people guidelines and models of dialogue. We do not seek "least common denominator Catholicism." Rather, we seek to help the faithful move beyond the often unnecessary and unhelpful polarization in our community and to refocus on the fundamental principles and pastoral needs of the church.

To move from the statement to the Catholic Common Ground Project, how would you describe its purpose? What activities will be involved?

It should be clear that our focus is pastoral, not doctrinal. We are not trying to change the church's teachings by some method of consensus or polling. We are primarily concerned with building up the church's unity by addressing many serious questions where Catholics may understandably disagree among themselves. These questions are not directly doctrinal, but they do require consideration of any doctrinal implications.

It is absolutely essential to understand that no one is equating the Catholic Common Ground Project with the church itself, nor are we equating the "revitalized common ground" we seek with the faith.

The Project will sponsor conferences and other reflections in which we will seek, as the opening paragraph states, "conditions for addressing our differences constructively," or as the statement later states, "a way" to understand and articulate discipleship in our time and place. We do not see ourselves as having a monopoly on this effort or even necessarily reaching collective positions. But, if the latter happens, we would not claim any special status for them.

Who will be involved in this effort?

First, I hope that many individuals and groups within the church will consider the statement to see if it suggests anything for their own work. Actually, this is already happening. Many have told us that they wish to take this effort into consideration in their parishes, colleges, deaneries, religious congregations, and other forums. We will have to consider how to help them do this.

In regard to the conferences or consultations sponsored by the Project, the advisory committee will be involved to the extent that their calendars and interest in the particular topics allow. We also hope to bring together many other people of diverse backgrounds and perspectives that will contribute to examination of the particular subject of each conference.

What will be discussed? Do you expect to discuss the issues that the media finds most divisive, such as abortion and women's ordination to the priesthood?

"Called to Be Catholic" lists a number of pastoral issues: changing roles of women, religious education, parish liturgy, human sexuality, the strain on dwindling numbers of priests, adequate formation for the increased number of lay persons in church leadership, the church in political life, the responsibility of theology to authoritative ecclesial teaching, and other issues. This list is a good place to start. These pastoral matters, regarding which the local church has responsibility, will be the object of our discussion. Present plans for the first conference focus on the church and U.S. culture.

As a realist, I expect that some participants will come to conferences holding positions at variance with ecclesial teaching or discipline regarding ordination, capital punishment, or any number of issues. But the role of authentic church teaching will always be clear and will be upheld.

Will the very fact of the conferences suggest that certain authoritative teachings are open to negotiation?

We cannot control how people interpret our effort, but the entire approach will be different from those efforts at mediation whose goal is simply compromise and false harmony.

What do you hope will be accomplished at the conferences?

Our hope is threefold. We hope that people of faith and leadership, whose divergent viewpoints have prevented them from listening adequately to one another, will have an opportunity to deepen and broaden their understanding of pastoral matters. Second, we hope that whatever emerges from these conferences in the way of publications will contribute to discussion in the larger church. Third, we hope to offer an example of how to engage in mutually respectful and constructive dialogue from which others might learn. As you can see, our goals are focused and modest.

How is this related to the National Conference of Catholic Bishops, and why wasn't the conference the forum for such an effort?

In the church there are numerous unofficial initiatives to address Catholic concerns. For example, there has been a recent and ongoing effort involving Catholic bishops and other individuals who issued a statement a few years ago that was intended to foster cooperation between Catholics and Evangelicals on matters of public policy. Moreover, the Catholic Campaign for America is an organization of prominent Catholics, which has the support of members of the hierarchy, but it is a public policy advocacy group independent of the official efforts of the bishops' conference. Pax Christi also brings together bishops and other Catholics in the effort to promote peace in the world. These are but three of a vast array of independent associations concerned about Catholic life. Our project is only another effort like these. The bishops' conference, on the other hand, is the official teaching and policy body of the Catholic Church in the United States.

Is it possible that the media can misuse this project to deepen divisions in the church or to suggest that the church should be guided by fluctuations in popular opinion?

Of course, this is true of all such projects. We are neither responsible for this result nor exempt from it, but we are trying to move beyond such manipulation by the way we drafted the statement and by the creation of forums where we can hear more clearly what is really being said.

What is the National Pastoral Life Center, and why is it involved?

The center is dedicated to serving our parishes and other forms of pastoral ministry through its publications, conferences, and research. It was begun thirteen years ago with the encouragement of the administrative committee of the U.S. bishops' conference and has served us well since. As I mentioned, the National Pastoral Life Center was involved from the beginning in the discussions that led to the statement and the project. The center's entire work has been to stimulate sound reflection and responsible action in parishes and dioceses in carrying out the church's pastoral mission. A majority of the bishops of our country have supported its work over the years, and I am confident they will continue to do so in coming years.

•

IN CONCLUSION, I assure you that I remain fully committed to this project. As I said at my press conference on August 12, "Our faith and our common life as members of the community of faith, which is the church, are indeed great and precious gifts. Let us together leave behind whatever brings discord. Let us recommit ourselves to this great heritage of faith."

I firmly believe that the ultimate test of this new initiative will be the one that Scripture proposes: If it is of God, it will bear fruit.

—

4

FAITHFUL AND HOPEFUL:
THE CATHOLIC COMMON GROUND PROJECT

Address by Joseph Cardinal Bernardin,
October 24, 1996

Two and a half months ago, I announced an initiative called the **Catholic Common Ground Project.** My aim was to help Catholics address, creatively and faithfully, questions that are vital if the church in the United States is to flourish as we enter the next millennium. At every level, we needed, I felt, to move beyond the distrust, the polarization, and the entrenched positions that have hampered our responses.

At the same time, I released a statement, "Called to Be Catholic: Church in a Time of Peril." Its very first paragraph

61

summed up what this initiative was about: "Will the Catholic Church in the United States enter the new millennium as a church of promise," it asked, or as "a church on the defensive"? The outcome, it proposed, depended on "whether American Catholicism can confront an array of challenges with honesty and imagination." "American Catholics," it stated, "must reconstitute the conditions for addressing our differences constructively." This can happen if we find a common ground. But not just any common ground. It has to be, as the statement said, "a common ground centered on faith in Jesus, marked by accountability to the living Catholic tradition, and ruled by a renewed spirit of civility, dialogue, generosity, and broad and serious consultation."

At that time, I also announced that I had assembled a committee of outstanding Catholics to join me in this Project—seven other bishops, including a fellow cardinal, five priests, three women religious, and eight lay men and women. They come from across the country, from diverse backgrounds in public service, intellectual life, business, and labor—and from a range of viewpoints regarding the needs of the church.

Although I felt that the statement "Called to Be Catholic" was an excellent description of our situation today, I did not ask these advisers to endorse its every word. I regret that some press reports mistakenly reported that committee members had signed the statement. My conviction, in fact, was that the words were not enough. The idea behind the **Catholic Common Ground Project** was to demonstrate how this call for a civil and generous dialogue, Christ-centered and accountable to the church's living tradition and teaching of the authentic magisterium, could be put into action.

To do that will take time, and at the end of August, as you well know, I discovered how little time remains for me personally. Earlier today, I met with the committee so that my role in this venture can be passed to others, and, this evening I am sharing these reflections with you in the hope that you too, in your own ways, will take up this task.

My thoughts this evening will cover several areas: the response to the Project, the reality of differences in the church, the relationship of the Project to doctrine and dissent, what is meant by the word "dialogue," and, finally, my hopes for the future of the Project.

RESPONSE

THE IMPORTANCE OF our task has been reinforced by the response that the announcement of the **Catholic Common Ground Project** has generated. I am not thinking so much of the public statements, for and against, that were widely reported in the media, although those, too, were welcome and valuable, even when unanticipated.

Rather, I am thinking of the outpouring of personal letters that have been sent to me and to the National Pastoral Life Center in New York—letters filled with words like "grateful," "heartening," "timely," "common sense," and even "joy." Priests and parishioners, women and men, recounted their frustrations and their fears that hope for the church was fading into deadlock or acrimony. Their letters also offered ideas, energy, institutional support. They reported discussions already being organized around "Called to Be Catholic." The letters were charged with the sense that something bottled up had been released, that something grown dormant was being reawakened.

Most of the letters avoided any note of triumphalism. They called, instead, for humility and prayerful reflection. Among the letter writers were some identifying themselves as conservatives and others calling themselves liberals, but both confessing that they had felt the acids of polarization, anger, and overreaction at work in their own souls.

There were, however, exceptions. A few people welcomed the Project, it seemed, as offering a new front or a promising arena in what they clearly viewed as little more than an ongoing battle within the church. But most, I am happy to say, seemed truly to feel the need to apply to themselves as well as to others the statement's call that we examine our situation with fresh eyes, open minds, and changed hearts.

If there was any frequent misunderstanding of the **Catholic Common Ground Project**, both among its supporters and its critics, it only reflected the church's current state of nervous anxiety. Some people hoped, and others feared, that this initiative would aim ambitiously at resolving all the church's major conflicts in our nation. Some seemed to imagine that the project planned to bring contending sides, like labor-management negotiators, to a bargaining table and somehow hammer out a new consensus on contentious issues within the church. In this misconception, the Common Ground Project's conferences would culminate in quasi-official reports or recommendations that had the potential to challenge or supplant the authority of diocesan bishops.

I apologize if any of my statements contributed to this impression. Precisely because this effort is so important to the hopes of so many, we need to be clear about the limits of this effort. Our aim is *not* to resolve all our differences or to establish a new ecclesial structure. Rather, it is, first of all, to learn how to make our differences fruitful. Agreements *may* emerge—all the better. But our first step is closer to what John Courtney Murray called the hard task of achieving genuine disagreement.

Common ground, in this sense, is not a new set of conclusions. It is a way of exploring our differences. It is a common spirit and ethic of dialogue. It is a space of trust set within boundaries. It is a place of respect where we can explore our differences, assured in the understanding that neither is everything "cut-and-dried" nor is everything "up for grabs."

DIFFERENCES

AS WE KNOW, differences have always existed in the church. St. Paul's letters and the Acts of the Apostles and the fact that there are four Gospel accounts rather than one all tell us that Christian unity has always coexisted with Christian differences. Differences are the natural reflection of our diversity, a diversity that comes with catholicity. Differences are the natural consequence of our grappling with a divine mystery that always remains beyond our complete comprehension. And differences, it must be added, can also spring from human sinfulness.

In the church's history, differences have often been the seedbeds of our most profound understanding of God and salvation. Differences and dissatisfaction have spurred extraordinary institutional creativity. And differences too often have provoked unnecessary, wasteful, and sometimes terrible, division.

What about today? By most historical standards the Catholic Church is not racked by overt divisions. Quite the contrary. No other global movement or body—political, religious, ideological—begins to approach the unity demonstrated time and again in the travels of the Holy Father whose remarkable pastoral leadership as shepherd and teacher has prepared us well for the new millennium and can be a helpful basis for the dialogue about which I will speak later. Our oneness in Spirit, our gathering from east to west at the eucharistic banquet, has never been rendered so visible to the human eye.

Yet, we have learned that in modern societies the greatest dangers may not manifest themselves so much in schism and rebellion as in hemorrhage and lassitude, complacency, the insidious draining of vitality, the haughty retreat into isolation, the dispiriting pressure of retrenchment. Secularization has triumphed where the church defaulted.

Are the differences among U.S. Catholics generating reflection, exchange, debate, ideas, initiative, decisiveness? Or are they producing distrust, polemics, weariness, withdrawal, inertia, deadlock?

No one can answer these questions definitively. But I and many others representing a range of theological outlooks feel that, in far too many cases, the brave new sparks and steady flame of vitality in the church are being smothered by the camps and distractions of our quarrels. The statement "Called to Be Catholic" described the situation realistically. "For three decades," it noted, "the church has been divided by different responses to the Second Vatican Council and to the tumultuous years that followed."

Despite the emergence of new generations with new questions, experiences, and needs, the statement continued, "party lines have hardened. A mood of suspicion and acrimony hangs over many of those most active in the church's life. . . . One consequence is that many of us are refusing to acknowledge disquieting realities, perhaps fearing that they may reflect poorly on our past efforts or arm our critics . . . Candid discussion is inhibited . . . Ideas, journals, and leaders are pressed to align themselves with pre-existing camps."

One could expand on that analysis. Rather than listen to an idea, we look for its "worst-case" extension; we suspect a hidden agenda. Anticipating attack, we avoid self-criticism and fear frank evaluation. We silence our doubts. We list the events of ecclesial life in parallel columns as wins or losses in a kind of zero-sum game.

I am almost embarrassed to give examples—first, because some of them are so painfully obvious and, second, because it is difficult to do so without inviting this process of testing for partisanship and hidden agendas. But let me mention only the very first item among the statement's examples of urgent questions that the church needs to address openly and honestly: "the changing roles of women." That would seem to be a rather obvious topic for examination, since the Holy Father has himself drawn our attention to it. Yet in the public responses to the statement, the fact that this question was listed first was enough to render our undertaking suspect by some, while the fact that it did not stipulate anything about ordination was a cause for rejection by others.

I believe that we long for a climate where a question as basic as this could be brought to the table in a mood of good will and with a readiness to learn from one another. We long to exchange ideas, informed by church teaching and witness, with a confidence that our heartfelt concerns for living the gospel faithfully will be heard and not slighted or betrayed.

CATHOLIC DOCTRINE

DO THE DIFFERENCES on topics like this have to do with Catholic doctrine, an area that is obviously less subject to change than pastoral practice? The question is significant. Some of the harshest criticisms of the **Catholic Common Ground Project** have arisen from anxiety that the exploration of differences could compromise the truth of Catholic doctrine. Such doctrine, it is said, already constitutes more than sufficient common ground, if only it were proclaimed without trepidation.

The answer to this question is twofold. First, many of the controversial differences among U.S. Catholics are not strictly doctrinal but, indeed, pastoral. The collaboration between clergy and laity in parish life, the effectiveness of religious education, the quality of liturgical celebration, the means of coping with declining number of priests and sisters —all the crucial areas pose numerous questions for which neither the *Catechism of the Catholic Church* nor the documents of Vatican II nor other magisterial sources provide precise and authoritative answers.

For example, in what sequence, and with what mixture of the affective and the conceptual, should the truths of the faith be introduced to children? How should religious education be structured around family life, sacramental preparation, classroom activities, the liturgy and its cycles? How should resources be distributed among Catholic schools, other forms of religious education, the family teaching moments of baptism, First Communion, marriage, and death? How should religious educators be formed, and programs realistically suited to volunteer teachers with high turnover rates? How can qualified lay professionals be identified, selected, sustained, and assured of respect and recompense in team ministries? What can be done to make the quality of homilies and congregational singing genuine assets in building a parish community?

To no small extent, the future vitality of the church hangs on such issues, and for concrete solutions we will not be able to rely solely on magisterial documents but will, instead, have to use our collective wisdom, knowledge, prudence, and sense of priorities.

But that is not the complete answer. There are doctrinal aspects to even the most pastoral of these questions, and these doctrinal aspects generate anxiety. It is both justified and imperative to ask what are the implications for doctrine of pastoral proposals or the implications for pastoral proposals of doctrine.

To ask such questions is more than an obligation. It is also an opportunity. Catholic doctrine provides enduring truths about divine and human reality. It should enlighten our minds, guide our daily actions, inform our spiritual striving. As we know, doctrine is often refined and nuanced, and is expressed as a carefully articulated structure rather than as an undifferentiated block. There also exists, as the Second Vatican Council stated, and the catechism repeats, a "hierarchy" of truths varying in their relation to the foundation of Christian faith. And Catholic belief is not static. Assisted by the Holy Spirit, the church is able to grow in its understanding of the heritage of faith. The *Catechism of the Catholic Church* is a gift to the Church because it is a compendium of this rich doctrinal heritage as it has developed over the centuries.

What is the practical import of this interlacing of the pastoral and the doctrinal? On the one hand, as "Called to Be Catholic" urges, "We should not rush to interpret disagreements as conflicts of starkly opposing principles rather than as differences in degree or in prudential pastoral judgments about the relevant facts." On the other hand, we must also "detect the valid insights and worries" embedded in our differing arguments. That being said, ultimately, our reflections and deliberations must be accountable to Scripture and tradition authentically interpreted—or in the words of the statement, to "the cloud of witnesses over the centuries or the living magisterium of the church exercised by the bishops and the Chair of Peter." On this point let there be no uncertainty!

DISSENT

YOU MAY HAVE noticed that so far I have spoken about differences without using the word "dissent." Some people have objected that the **Catholic Common Ground Project** will legitimate dissent, and others, perhaps, have hoped that it will. In part, I have addressed this concern by noting the range of differences among U.S. Catholics that are not strictly or primarily doctrinal. But dissent, in addition, is a complicated term. I mean neither to avoid it nor to pretend to address all the issues surrounding it.

One can find, however, some major points of consensus about dissent.

On the one hand, consider the view that all public disagreement or criticism of church teaching is illegitimate. Such an unqualified understanding is unfounded and would be a disservice to the church. "Room must be made for responsible dissent in the church," writes Father Avery Dulles, whom no one can accuse of being radical or reckless in his views. "Theology always stands under correction."

"Dissent should neither be glorified nor be vilified," Father Dulles adds. It inevitably risks weakening the church as a sign of unity, but it can nonetheless be justified, and to suppress it would be harmful. "The good health of the church demands continual revitalization by new ideas," Father Dulles says, adding that "nearly every creative theologian has at one time or another been suspected of corrupting the faith." In fact, according to Dulles, theologians ought to alert church authorities to the shortcomings of its teachings.

Similarly, in *Veritatis Splendor* Pope John Paul II distinguished between "limited and occasional dissent" and "an overall and systematic calling into question of traditional moral doctrine." I would argue that dissent ceases to be legitimate when it takes the form of aggressive public campaigns against church teachings that undermine the authority of the magisterium itself.

No one can deny that such campaigns exist. But I would go further. The problem of dissent today is not so much the voicing of serious criticism but the popularity of dismissive, demagogic, "cute" commentary, dwelling on alleged motives, exploiting stereotypes, creating stock villains, employing reliable "laugh lines." The kind of responsible disagreement of which I speak must not include "caricatures" that "undermine the church as a community of faith" by assuming church authorities to be "generally ignorant, self-serving, and narrow-minded." It takes no more than a cursory reading of the more militant segments of the Catholic press, on both ends of the theological and ideological spectrum, to reveal how widespread, and how corrosive, such caricatures have become.

This is why the **Catholic Common Ground Project,** while affirming "legitimate debate, discussion, and diversity," specifically targets "pop scholarship, sound-bite theology, unhistorical assertions, and flippant dismissals." Moreover, it aims at giving Catholics another model for exploring our differences. Before speaking of that model I want to make it clear that, in speaking of a "common ground," this Project does not aim at the lowest common denominator. Nor when it speaks of dialogue does it imply compromise. Rather, in both instances its goal is the fullest possible understanding of and internalization of the truth.

DIALOGUE

THE PROJECT'S MODEL is dialogue. But we have done more than merely invoke that word. Unfortunately, the call for dialogue has too often become routine, a gambit in the wars of image-making, a tactic in reopening or prolonging bureaucratic negotiations. Nonetheless the recognition and highlighting of dialogue remains one of the glories of the Second Vatican Council and of the papacies that nurtured and followed it. In dialogue we affirm, examine, deepen, and rectify our own defining beliefs in relationship to another person. That relationship involves opposition but also sincere respect, trust, and expectation of mutual enrichment.

The statement "Called to Be Catholic" proposes conditions for a renewed and successful dialogue among U.S. Catholics. Let us remind ourselves of a few of them:

1. that Jesus Christ, present in Scripture and sacrament, be central to all that we do;
2. that we reaffirm basic truths and stand accountable to Scripture and Catholic tradition, witnessed and conveyed to us by the Spirit-filled, living church and

its magisterium exercised by the bishops and the Chair of Peter;

3. that the complexity and richness of this tradition not be reduced or ignored by fundamentalist appeals to a text or a decree and or by narrow appeals to individual or contemporary experience;

4. that the church be treated not as a merely human organization but as a communion, a spiritual family, requiring that a hermeneutic of suspicion be balanced by a hermeneutic of love and retrieval, and that Catholic leadership embrace wide and serious consultation;

5. that our discussions assume the need for boundaries, distinctions, and defining limits, even where these may be open to reexamination;

6. that we recognize no single group as possessing a monopoly on solutions to the church's problems or the right to spurn the mass of Catholics and their leaders as unfaithful;

7. that we test proposals for pastoral realism;

8. that we presume those with whom we differ to be in good faith and put the best possible construction on their positions;

9. that, above all, we keep the liturgy, our common worship, from becoming a battleground for confrontation and polarization.

HOPES

I TRUST THAT these reflections have been of some help in our coming to a better understanding of the Project and its direction. Now allow me some personal thoughts.

Shortly after the Project was announced, a friend asked me, "Joe, why at this time in your life did you take on this Project?" My friend was referring to the stress of the last three years, in particular the stress of a false accusation and then of being a cancer patient. It was a good question. It prompted me to reflect more deeply about my many life experiences and my own spiritual journey.

I thought immediately of the lessons I had learned from my mentors, Archbishop Paul Hallinan of Atlanta and John Cardinal Dearden of Detroit: to trust that, through open and honest dialogue, differences could be resolved and the gospel proclaimed in its integrity. Over the years I learned from you and so many other of our sisters and brothers the correctness of what these two great churchmen taught me. I have been impressed and humbled by the willingness of so many to rise above differences in search for the truth that can bind us together. I have been nurtured by the peace and joy of communities that have worked hard for reconciliation and peace.

This same insight prompted me to move beyond the family of faith and speak to our society about a consistent ethic of life. In asking opponents of abortion and opponents of capital punishment and nuclear war to perceive a whole spectrum of life-issues not in identical terms but, rather, in relationship to one another, I have been moved by the conviction that the church's understanding of the gospel defies conventional political and ideological lines. By juxtaposing positions that are conventionally set apart and by searching for the common thread, we enrich our own understanding and open others to persuasion.

Similarly, the **Catholic Common Ground Project** offers the promise of our rising above hardened party lines and finding renewal in the splendor of the truth revealed in the person of Jesus who is our Lord and our savior.

This evening, I assure you that, having entered the final phase of my life's journey, I am even more committed than before to this central conviction. A dying person does not have time for the peripheral or the accidental. He or she is drawn to the essential, the important—yes, the eternal. And what is important, my friends, is that we find that unity with the Lord and within the community of faith for which Jesus prayed so fervently on the night before he died. To say it quite boldly, it is wrong to waste the precious gift of the time given to us, as God's chosen servants, on acrimony and division.

And so, in that spirit I hand on to you the gift that was given to me—a vision of the church that trusts in the power of the Spirit so much that it can risk authentic dialogue. I hand that gift on to you without fear or trepidation. I say this because I know that it is a gift you already prize and cherish. I ask you, without waiting and on your own, to strengthen the common ground, to examine our situation with fresh eyes, open minds, and changed hearts, and to confront our challenges with honesty and imagination. Guided by the Holy Spirit, together, we can more effectively respond to the challenges of our times as we carry forward the mission that the Lord Jesus gave to us, his disciples. It is to promote that mission that the constructive dialogue we seek is so important.

IN ADDITION, I ASK you to read carefully "Called to Be Catholic." Like some of the committee, you may not agree with every sentence or paragraph. But ask yourself carefully where and why you agree or disagree. Discuss it in your families, your parishes, your schools. Make it the occasion for a serious examination of conscience and not for further contention.

Then, I ask you to go a step further. Whether you are guided by this statement or similar principles, please decide how it might modify the conduct or the tone of whatever group efforts engage you in the church—your parish council, your prayer group, your Catholic grade school or high school faculty, your academic department or professional organization if these deal with religious issues. Are these the principles—the centrality of Jesus, the serious accountability to church tradition and authentic teaching, the spirit of dialogue and consultation—that govern the Catholic periodicals you read, the television programs you watch, the organizations to which you belong, or the conferences you attend? If not, make your preferences known.

As you do this, return to the teachings of the Second Vatican Council, which I believe with all my being was the work of God's Holy Spirit. While there is so much in conciliar teaching that can guide these efforts, you might find inspiration in a passage at the close of *Gaudium et Spes*, the Pastoral Constitution on the Church in the Modern World. This passage calls on the church to become a sign of sincere dialogue as part of its mission to enlighten the world with the gospel's message and unite all people in the one Spirit. I close with the inspiring words of that passage: "Such a mission," the council fathers instructed,

> requires us first of all to create in the Church itself mutual esteem, reverence and harmony, and acknowledge all legitimate diversity; in this way all who constitute the one people of God will be able to engage in ever more fruitful dialogue, whether they are pastors or

other members of the faithful. For the ties which unite the faithful together are stronger than those which separate them: let there be unity in what is necessary, freedom in what is doubtful, and charity in everything. (no. 92)

5

DIALOGUE:
A LABOR IN LOVE

Address by
Archbishop Oscar H. Lipscomb,
March 7, 1997

Let me begin by saying once again how good it is for us to be together for this inaugural conference of the Catholic Common Ground Initiative. I am deeply appreciative of the efforts of so many who labored to bring this about in a rather brief period of time. Likewise, I want to express my gratitude to those of you who accepted the invitation to join with the advisory committee for this meeting. Your willingness to come on short notice reflects your deep commitment to the church and its well-being.

Before moving into my formal remarks I hope that you will indulge me a few personal thoughts. It was last summer when Cardinal Bernardin first contacted me about participating in what at that time he called the Catholic Common Ground Project. Obviously to be invited to assist the Cardinal in any project would have been an honor. You know, as well as I, how important his servant leadership was to the church. Equally important, however, was the substance of the project. Though I, along with some of you, might have wished to enhance or nuance certain aspects of the foundational document, "Called to Be Catholic: Church in a Time of Peril," I felt then, and still feel today, that the Initiative is something that is needed by the church in the United States. Consequently I enthusiastically accepted his invitation to serve on the advisory committee and looked forward to its first meeting quite mindful of the Cardinal's assurance that service on the advisory committee would not be an onerous responsibility.

None of us had expected that the Cardinal's health would deteriorate so quickly. Thus it was quite a surprise when he called in mid-October to ask me to succeed him as chair of the committee. How could I say no? At the same time, however, how could I say yes? I knew all too well that Cardinal Bernardin was a person not easily succeeded. I also was aware that the committee he had gathered was composed of individuals any one of whom could have been a successful chair.

In the end I said yes in the hope that by accepting the Cardinal's invitation I might in my own small way keep this legacy alive in the church he loved and served so well. As I said good-bye to him before his funeral, I promised him that I would do my best and asked that he pray for all of us as we move forward. I am sure that he is with us today.

In my remarks this evening I would like to do three things. First, I want to situate this meeting in the context of the lively discussion that has taken place about the document "Called to Be Catholic" and the Initiative. Second, I would like to talk a bit about the word "dialogue" as it has been used in church documents. Finally, I would like to offer some personal and pastoral thoughts about how we might engage in our pursuit of an authentically Catholic common ground.

Previous Discussions

IN PREPARING FOR this gathering, I spent time reviewing some of what has been written about this Initiative. If success is to be gauged by the quantity of words written, then we have been quite successful. For the sake of conversation I would suggest that there have been three stages to the discussion of the Initiative.

The first stage consisted of the initial comments and statements, including those of some of my brother bishops. As you know a number of those comments expressed serious reservations. In rereading some of the statements it seems to me that they can be characterized as expressing concerns about what they perceived "Called to Be Catholic" to be saying. The context for these perceptions was a very real concern for the pastoral well being of the church. It was, simply, that "Called to Be Catholic" and the Project might do more harm than good.

Cardinal Bernardin responded to those concerns on August 29 by issuing a press statement and a 10-page document that sought to address the questions that had been raised. He continued to engage the question in his address at the inaugural Catholic Common Ground Initiative event on October 24. He reminded us that the common ground we sought, as "Called to Be Catholic" noted, was to be "a common ground centered on faith in Jesus, marked by accountability to the living Catholic tradition, and ruled by a renewed spirit of civility, dialogue, generosity, and broad and serious consultation."

Much of his response clarified what had already been said in order that our critics might have a better understanding of the true nature of the Initiative. In effect, he said that there is no reason to fear that the Catholic Common Ground Initiative will do harm to the family of faith. This point was made most passionately when the Cardinal challenged us, as perhaps only a dying person could, to "find that unity with the Lord and within the community of faith for which Jesus prayed so fervently on the night before he died." He went on to say, in his words "quite boldly" that "it is wrong to waste the precious gift of time given to us, as God's chosen servants, on acrimony and division."

The second stage of discussion has been centered, I believe, on what others would suggest the text "implies." These critics propose that when the text is read in the current cultural and ecclesial context, it is reasonable that people could come to conclusions that are not part of the formal text. Foremost among those sharing this perspective is the distinguished Jesuit theologian Father Avery Dulles. In the Ninth Annual Fall Laurence J. McGinley Lecture at Fordham University ("The Travails of Dialogue," *Origins*, November 16, 1996), Father Dulles noted that his difficulty was not so much with what the statement said as with what it "seemed to imply, and would be understood as implying in the current atmosphere."

In my reading of Dulles's remarks I certainly resonated with his concerns about a "privatized church" and the need to have realistic expectations about both the nature of and the results of dialogue. It is important that any proposal for dialogue, as he noted, "be very carefully formulated if it is not to expand the zone of disagreement within the church."

Father Robert Imbelli, who is with us today, wrote a quite thoughtful and respectful reply to the McGinley lecture. It was printed in the *National Catholic Register* (December 22–28, 1996). He noted that before being a call to dialogue, "Called to Be Catholic" is a call to discernment and conversion; to "examine our situation with fresh eyes, open minds, and changed hearts." And the goal of such discernment and of any dialogue it may promote is "to understand for ourselves and articulate for our world the meaning of discipleship of Jesus Christ." He went on to point out one of the statement's most powerful affirmations: "Jesus Christ, present in Scripture and sacrament, is central to all that we do; he must always be the measure and not what is measured."

While the first stage of reactions was based on perceptions and the second stage focused on implications that could be taken from the text, the third stage is now addressing what its critics believe the *text failed to say*. To be honest I find this stage to be the most intriguing, because in many ways I believe it leads us to some of the most neuralgic issues we face as church. It also is the most difficult stage to date. This is because what is being discussed is not the absence of necessary foundational principles but how they are to be understood and how they are ordered and integrated into the foundational document "Called to Be Catholic." A document that was proposed as an analytic instrument to facilitate an enhancement of the pastoral life of the church is being subject to a theological scrutiny it was never intended to sustain. That being said, it is important that we acknowledge that we have entered this new stage and respond to it as best we can.

Before doing that, however, I do want to take note of a subject that has been present implicitly and explicitly during all three of these stages, a subject that was addressed quite clearly by Cardinal Ratzinger in an address to bishops from mission territories last September. The *Origins* title of the text was "Relativism: The Central Problem of Faith Today" (vol. 26: no. 20, Oct. 31, 1996). As always, the text reveals both the breadth of the Cardinal's knowledge and the universality of his pastoral concerns. His remarks engage Kant, Marx, Hick, Asian religion, New Age theories, liberation theology, Marxism, and scriptural exegesis, to name but some of the topics.

In his comments the Cardinal states quite clearly that

> relativism has thus become the central problem for the faith at the present time. No doubt it is not presented only with its aspects of resignation before the immensity of the truth. It is also presented as a position defined positively by the concepts of tolerance and knowledge through dialogue and freedom, concepts which would be limited if the existence of one valid truth for all were affirmed. (p. 311)

Having identified the problem of relativism, the Cardinal then discusses its impact on theology in general and Christology in particular. It is in this context that he then speaks of the notion of dialogue. He argues that when relativism becomes a tenet of theology

> the notion of *dialogue*—which has maintained a position of significant importance in the Platonic and

Christian tradition—changes meaning and becomes both the quintessence of the relativist creed and the antithesis of conversion and mission. In the relativist meaning, *to dialogue* means to put one's own position, i.e., one's faith, on the same level as the convictions of others without recognizing in principle more truth in it than what is attributed to the opinion of others. (p. 312; italics in original)

I believe it is important that all of us study the Cardinal's remarks. His concerns are well founded and, as I noted above, are shared by many of our critics. It could well explain why our use of the word "dialogue" has aroused such concern. For our critics the word is a loaded one. In fact one might wonder whether it carries "so much baggage" that its usage is counterproductive. While such wonderment is understandable, I would suggest that we continue to use the word. Cardinal Ratzinger uses it himself in the same address when he calls for "efforts toward a new dialogue . . . between faith and philosophy" (p. 316). What is imperative, however, is that we continue to affirm what was said in "Called to Be Catholic," namely, that in the dialogue of which we speak, "Jesus Christ, present in Scripture and sacrament, is central to all that we do" and that all dialogue is accountable to Scripture and to the Catholic tradition, witnessed and conveyed to us by "the Spirit filled, living Church and its magisterium exercised by the bishops and the Chair of Peter." Ours is not the dialogue of relativism but of fidelity.

That being said we now can consider some of the specifics of this third stage of critique. It is outlined quite well in David Schindler's article in *Communio* entitled "On the Catholic Common Ground Project: The Christological Foundations of Dialogue" (vol. 23, no. 4, Winter 1996).

There is something refreshing about Schindler's text in that he does affirm that "Called to Be Catholic" and the Cardinal's subsequent statements reflect orthodox commitments. As he wrote: "The National Pastoral Life Center's statement does in fact contain all the elements necessary for an adequate christology and ecclesiology—Cardinal Bernardin and Father Imbelli are right about this" (pp. 828–29). What the text fails to do for Schindler is properly to "integrate these doctrinal assumptions into its conceptions of dialogue, precisely at those critical junctures where authentically Catholic and unacceptably liberal conceptions of dialogue are most apt to be confused" (p. 829). This critique, however, is not meant to demean "the Catholicity of the Cardinal's intention" or the good faith of the Cardinal "and those associated with the statement" (p. 829).

In this environment of good will Schindler raises a variety of concerns which I cannot adequately represent in these brief remarks. Clearly he shares the concerns expressed by Cardinal Ratzinger and others about the limits and even dangers of what is described as our liberal cultural context. He clearly desires that any true dialogue not just be a subjective experience of process but that it be grounded in an objectivity that is substantial in nature. Similarly an authentic common ground must be substantive and not just a matter of form. The a prioris that determine both the content and the process of dialogue must be sacramental, hierarchical, and ontological in nature and not contractual, sociological, and moral. The existential condition of those who participate in dialogue is not to be understood in an overly optimistic manner. The need for forgiveness is not something extrinsic but intrinsic. Sin and redemption, the need for conversion, and the call to sanctity are essential components of authentic dialogue. The peril, the polarization that the church faces, is not just something that is horizontal in nature; it is not just a breakdown in communication between discrete individuals. Rather it is a polarization of individuals "who have already been constituted, in and by Jesus Christ, into a sacramental–ontological unity" (p. 843). The peril, the polarization, of necessity has a vertical dimension.

In the conclusion to his argument Schindler notes that

> it is the question regarding the basic nature of our current polarization and of authentic dialogue that is itself the most significant source of polarization and of the absence of authentic dialogue. The fundamental question, the question that has provoked the most attention and the deepest disagreement concerns precisely the christological and indeed ecclesiological nature of our polarization—of the critical issues facing the Church—and of the methods deemed most effective in addressing these. (p. 849)

He goes on to say that what is at issue is the meaning to be ascribed to the centrality of Christ. He postulates that "the dispute bears not on whether we should, a priori, assume a community among us in Christ (who would deny this?), but how we are to understand this prior, anterior community" (ibid.).

Obviously Schindler has posed some quite substantive concerns. It is my hope that in the course of time those here present and others will be able to engage in reasoned discourse with what he has written.

As you no doubt have noted, I have chosen not to engage in a detailed refutation of these three stages of critique. Rather, it is my intention to take note of them in a formal manner. I do so not that they might be dismissed but that they might be seen as worthy opportunities to carry forward in the spirit of Cardinal Bernardin. If we are to be faithful to his vision, then we must treat our critics with the utmost respect and respond with an openness that seeks only to find the splendor of the truth.

Now, I would like to offer a few observations, more pastoral in nature, to the three levels of critique. As for the first stage of *perception*, I am confident, as Schindler has noted, that both the foundational document and the Initiative are not at variance with authentic church teaching and do, in fact, represent a deep fidelity to and love for the communion of faith that is the church. It is important, however, that we attend to the concerns of bishops and others about how this Initiative might be misused or unwittingly become the source of discord within particular churches. While we are not responsible for the actions of others not associated with us, we must do all that we can to serve the cause of authentic church unity.

Turning to the second stage, what some might conclude the text *implies*, I believe we must be more sensitive to our cultural and ecclesial context. I am sure that all of us have been amazed at what people have read the text to be saying or justifying. Clearly the "eye of the beholder" has at times found what the authors of the text never intended. I believe it is important that all of us, with the same gentle but firm manner of the Cardinal, point out that some of the implications taken from the text, quite simply, are incorrect. In that vein I find it quite problematic that some public officials have been using the words of Cardinal Bernardin written for the Initiative in the context of their support for abortion. This does a great disservice to the memory of the Cardinal—a person whose commitment to the cause of life, and most especially the life of the unborn, is without question.

As for the third stage which discusses *integration and prioritization*, I would suggest that it points out the need for this conference on the relationship between church and culture. Dulles, Schindler, and others clearly have a theological perspective on our Western culture and considered opinions on how best to approach it. It is important that we attend to these perspectives and provide the requested theological analysis. As we engage in this analysis we also must become more explicit about our own christological and ecclesiological a prioris. This might be one of the most fruitful outcomes of this third stage of discussion. At the same time, however, we cannot be consumed with "converting" our critics. I suspect that when one enters a world as nebulous as the ordering and integrating of theological concepts unanimity might never be realized.

THE MEANING OF DIALOGUE

IN REVIEWING THE various stages of critique of the Initiative, I noted the concern raised about the Initiative's use of the word "dialogue." Because of the centrality of this concept to both our project and our critics, I would like to spend some time reviewing how the word has been used in ecclesial circles.

Though we all know that the word "dialogue" has been a part of church life since the time of the Second Vatican Council, the word has been used with different meanings in different contexts. For example, "dialogue" is often used as an image of prayer (e.g., *Directory on the Ministry and Life of Priests*, no. 5: The priest must live his vocation "in a dialogue of adoration and of love with the three divine persons"). In liturgical discussions "dialogue" means the ritual dialogue between celebrant and people. Sometimes "dialogue" is used to speak of open and compassionate relationships between teachers and students (e.g., education is described in *Vita Consecrata* [1993] as a "dialogue with young women and men so as to form them after the heart of Christ") or parents and children (no. 49 in *Educational Guidance in Human Love*).

At other times "dialogue" is used to mean consultation to gain information from others (e.g., *Communio et Progressio* [1971 Pastoral Instruction on Social Communications], 122: "The Church does not speak and listen to her own members alone; her dialogue is with the whole world. . . . She is to 'read the signs of the times,' for these too reveal the message of God and indicate the unfolding of the history of salvation under divine providence").

Perhaps the best theological description of dialogue is to be found in Pope Paul VI's encyclical letter *Ecclesiam Suam*. In fact, part three of that document is entitled "The Dialogue" and is a sustained reflection on the need for dialogue if the church is to carry out its mission of evangelization in the modern world.

Paul VI speaks of the "transcendent origin of the dialogue. It is found in the very plan of God. Religion, of its very nature, is a relationship between God and man. Prayer expresses such a relationship in dialogue. . . . The history of salvation narrates exactly this long and changing dialogue which begins with God and brings to man a many-splendored conversation" (no. 70).

Later in that document Paul VI says:

> In the dialogue one discovers how different are the ways which lead to the light of faith, and how it is possible to make them converge on the same goal. Even if these ways

are divergent they can become complementary by forcing our reasoning process out of the worn paths and by obliging it to deepen its research to find fresh expressions.

The dialectic of this exercise of thought and patience will make us discover elements of truth also in the opinions of others, it will force us to express our teachings with great fairness, and it will reward us for the work of having explained it in accordance with the objections of another or despite his slow assimilation of our teaching. The dialogue will make us wise; it will make us teachers. (no. 83)

The bishops of the Second Vatican Council expressed the same themes when they wrote with enthusiasm in *Gaudium et Spes* about the importance of dialogue to the mission of the church.

By virtue of her mission to shed on the whole world the radiance of the Gospel message, and to unify under one Spirit all men of whatever nation, race or culture, the Church stands forth as a sign of that brotherhood which allows honest dialogue and gives it vigor.

Such a mission requires in the first place that we foster within the Church herself mutual esteem, reverence and harmony, through the full recognition of lawful diversity. Thus all those who compose the one people of God, both pastors and the general faithful, can engage in dialogue with ever abounding fruitfulness. For the bonds which unite the faithful are mightier than anything dividing them. Hence, let there be unity in what is necessary, freedom in what is unsettled, and charity in any case. (*Gaudium et Spes*, 92)

Another significant discussion of dialogue is found in *Communio et Progressio*. Allow me to digest some of its more salient points:

Communication and dialogue among Catholics are indispensable. . . . Those who exercise authority in the church will take care to ensure that there is reasonable exchange of freely held and expressed opinion among the people of God. . . . It must be taken that the truths of faith express the essence of the Church and therefore do not leave room for arbitrary interpretations. Nonetheless the Church moves with the movement of man. She therefore has to adapt herself to the special circumstances that arise out of time and place. She has to consider how the truths of the faith may be explained in different times and cultures. She has to reach a multitude of decisions while adjusting her actions to the changes around her. While the individual Catholic follows the magisterium, he can and should engage in free research so that he may better understand revealed truths or explain them to a society subject to incessant change. (nos. 114–17)

The document moves from this more generic discussion of dialogue with the world to discuss dialogue within the church:

This free dialogue within the church does no injury to her unity and solidarity. It nurtures concord and the meeting of minds by permitting the free play of the variations of public opinion. But in order that this dialogue may go in the right direction it is essential that charity is in command even when there are differing views. Everyone in this dialogue should be animated by the desire to serve and to consolidate unity and cooperation. There should be a desire to build and not to destroy. There should be a deep love for the church and a compelling desire for its unity. Christ made love the sign by which men can recognize his true church and therefore his true followers. (no. 117)

I know that I have spent a good deal of time citing ecclesial documents. My reason for such extensive quoting was not to gain credibility for our venture, to wrap, so to speak, the Initiative in the cloak of magisterial texts, but to seek guidance for ourselves and others as we move forward, to find a truly Catholic common ground for the concept of dialogue.

PASTORAL REFLECTION

THIS LEADS ME to the third, final and shortest part of my remarks tonight. As I did in the earlier section, I would like to spend a few moments with you reflecting on our Initiative and its proposed dialogue as a pastor. In a sense what follows is more of a pastoral reflection than a theological discussion. The foundation for this reflection is, however, what we have just heard in the texts I have cited. It also engages some of what our critics have written.

All of us are profoundly aware of the impact of the Enlightenment on first world culture and, eventually, on the life of the church. With the "turn to the subject," the traditional reference point of first world philosophy shifted. While it would be true to say that in many ways the church rejected this shift, in time, especially since the Second World War, the church has engaged in its own dialogue with contemporary philosophy and culture. That dialogue, I would suggest, has been guided or informed by numerous givens or non-negotiables which are essential to our ecclesial heritage. I will mention but a few.

First, there has been the conviction that there is an "objectivity" an "out-thereness" which is the proper subject of theological reflection: An objectivity that is "received" and not created. Second, dialogue is pursued in the context of community in which the human subject is able to overcome alienation and despair. A community that is itself an objective reality and not just a functional entity created by human intentionality. In sustaining these convictions this dialogue has refused to accept an eclipse of ultimate mystery and radical transcendence. This ecclesial dialogue has been about *fides quaerens intellectum*. In a phrase, it has been dialogue that is a graced participation in mystery.

It is such a graced participation in mystery of individuals within the *communio*, the communion of faith, that is the only authentic foundation for our Catholic Common Ground Initiative.

But where do we turn to enable such a dialogue? How can we ensure that our efforts will be animated by the deep love and desire for unity about which our ecclesial documents speak so forcefully?

Each of you might have your own answer to these questions. My answer is quite simple: Our dialogue must find its basis in that common prayer which is the liturgy, the "work" of the church. We are all aware of the ancient affirmation *lex orandi, lex credendi*. Pope John Paul II implies a third category which we might call *lex agendi* as a result of encounter with Christ's sacrificial love. It also has a place in our dialogue. In *Tertio Millennio Adveniente* the Holy Father noted that one effect of the church's public worship is to inspire a "true longing for holiness, a deep desire for conversion and personal renewal in a context of ever more intense prayer and of solidarity with one's neighbor, especially the most needy" (no. 42).

That same imperative was considered by Cardinal Bernardin in a pastoral letter on the liturgy which, unfortunately, he was not able to complete. In one part of this draft letter he was reflecting on the relationship between liturgy and catechesis. I believe his words speak to our Initiative:

> I want to invite us to a restoration. Not a restoration of a past that really only exists in nostalgia, but to a sense of the unity of liturgy and catechesis. The homilist, the presider, the liturgist and the catechist are those who enter into the holy of holies, who encounter the full mystery that is God in liturgy and from that experience are able to speak of it in homily and religious education. As the Council taught us, full participation in the liturgy "is the primary, indeed the indispensable source from which the Christian faithful are to derive the true Christian spirit" (*Constitution on the Sacred Liturgy*, 4). Thus it is that the liturgist, the catechist, and most especially the homilist share the responsibility of challenging us again and again to build our bridges between the source of our spirit and its expression in the world where we live. Without the regular celebration of a full participatory liturgy, preaching, and catechesis we have nothing to say, no source, no ground. And so we will never achieve our objective: living lives that are spent in justice and good work.

Ours is an Initiative that seeks to build bridges "between those who have differing perspectives on the relationship between the source of our spirit and its expression." As we seek something to say, as we seek a source for authentic dialogue, then I think we must attend to Monsignor Velo's eloquent turn of phrase in his funeral homily. He told us that Cardinal Bernardin had taught us that common ground is holy ground. It is the *mysterium tremendum* encountered in the transforming experience of the church's public worship that provides our dialogue with its source and its goal. It is this encounter with Christ's sacrificial love poured out that allows us as sinners to be forgiven in order to be about God's work. It is this liturgical *epiclesis* that calls forth the Spirit that binds us together as one family and fills us with the fire of love.

If the common ground that we seek in our Initiative is truly grace-filled ground, then we and our critics will have nothing to fear. Ours will not be an experience of mere theological discourse but truly a labor of love in service to God's truth. A labor that, by his blessing and our efforts, is conducted in space made holy.